Sound Advice on

Mastering

D1559464

by Bill Gibson

ProAudio
press

447 Georgia Street
Vallejo, CA 94590
(707) 554-1935

Publisher: Mike Lawson
Art Director: Stephen Ramirez; Editor: Patrick Runkle
Cover image Gregg Field Studio City, ©Edward Colver,
studio design by studio bau:ton.

ProAudio Press is an imprint of artistpro.com, LLC
447 Georgia Street
Vallejo, CA 94590
(707) 554-1935

Also from ProMusic Press
Music Copyright for the New Millennium
The Mellotron Book
Electronic Music Pioneers

Also from EMBooks
The Independent Working Musician
Making the Ultimate Demo, 2nd Ed.
Remix: The Electronic Music Explosion
Making Music with Your Computer, 2nd Ed.
Anatomy of a Home Studio
The EM Guide to the Roland VS-880

Also from MixBooks
The AudioPro Home Recording Course, Volumes I, II, and III
The Art of Mixing: A Visual Guide to Recording, Engineering, and Production
The Mixing Engineer's Handbook
The Mastering Engineer's Handbook
Music Publishing: The Real Road to Music Business Success, Rev. and Exp. 5th Ed.
How to Run a Recording Session
The Professional Musician's Internet Guide
The Songwriters Guide to Collaboration, Rev. and Exp. 2nd Ed.
Critical Listening and Auditory Perception
Modular Digital Multitracks: The Power User's Guide, Rev. Ed.
Professional Microphone Techniques
Sound for Picture, 2nd Ed.
Music Producers, 2nd Ed.
Live Sound Reinforcement
Professional Sound Reinforcement Techniques
Creative Music Production: Joe Meek's Bold Techniques

Printed in Auburn Hills, MI
ISBN 1-931140-35-9

Contents

What Is Mastering? 5

To Master or Not to Master 8

Acoustic Considerations 12

Monitoring 16

Digital versus Analog..21

Mastering to Error Correcting Recorders 23

Digital Modeling 29

Cabling Considerations 30

Assembling the Album...42

Equalizing 44

Real-time Analyzer (RTA) 50

Levels..54

Limiting: How to Sound Loud 58

How Hot Is Hot Enough?...60

The CD Mastering Environment...62

Image Files 76

Summary 77

What Is Mastering?

Mastering is the final preparation of music for duplication. In today's music world, that most often means taking mixdowns from the studio, optimizing the sound of each track, then arranging the mastered tracks on a replication-ready format—such as a CD-R—that will be used to manufacture the final product. Optimizing the sound of each track entails many technical considerations and many subjective choices, all based on the experience and taste of the mastering engineer. The commanding, punchy sound of the latest hit mix has much to do with the original recording, but it also has a lot to do with the mastering process.

The mastering engineer listens for consistent levels from song to song. If a song or two is slightly louder or softer than the rest, levels will be matched.

This is also the point where global equalization might take place. If one song sounds weak in low-frequency content, for example, the mastering engineer selects the low frequency to boost, which helps the deficient song match the others in overall sound. These equalization moves typically affect the entire mix in an identical way on both channels of the stereo mix.

Limiting and compression are commonly used during mastering. A hard limiter lets the engineer add decibels to the overall mix level. If the limiter registers a 6dB reduction in gain during the mix and the levels are optimized so as to achieve a maximum signal level, the mix has been made 6dB louder in comparison to its pre-limiting status. That's typically very good, since commercial music is often compared in relation to how loud it sounds in a broadcast, dance, or environmental application. When a song is effectively louder, it is typically perceived as stronger and more appealing than the songs heard before or after it.

Sound Advice on Mastering

The mastering engineer also takes into consideration the flow of the album. A good engineer creates a flow where the songs actually grow slightly in level. This pulls the listener more effectively through the album. If the songs grow in perceived volume throughout the album, even if it's nearly imperceptible, the listener follows the musical progress from beginning to end more comfortably.

This creation of continuity and flow doesn't only include level. It might involve a bit more limiting toward the end of the album, which can make an apparently constant level sound as if it's increasing— the songs at the end will seem louder even though their peak levels are the same as that of the early songs.

Spacing between songs can also be decided during mastering. Most songs flow best with two to four seconds between them. However, there should be continuity and flow considerations that drive the decisions on spacing between songs. If a very fast song follows a very slow song, it's typically a good idea to leave a little more space after the slow song just to let the listener settle down. On the other hand, some songs want to fade directly into each other.

When adjusting spacing between songs, listen to the transitions to verify how comfortably they flow. Even if you don't quite know why, you'll be able to discern much about the effectiveness of the transition from one song to the next.

To Master or Not to Master

With today's technology, anybody can prepare his or her musical product for duplication. You can send a master that will serve as the production master for your final product. You can compress, limit, equalize, effect, shorten, lengthen, space, and insert subcodes and indexes all from the comfort of your bedroom studio. However, should you? What's the advantage to doing your own mastering at home? What's the advantage to sending your work out be mastered by someone else in another facility? How can you develop the skills needed to do a good job of mastering?

Should you do your own mastering?
I believe the answer to this question is entirely subject to the goal of the project. If you're recording your best buddy's band, they just want a product they can sell at their gigs, and they're down-and-out broke, go ahead and master the album yourself. However, do it in a way that is instructive. Research the best way to work with the equipment and software you're using. Research the art of mastering. Try different versions of your work and, above all, compare your work to the real world.

What's the advantage to doing your own mastering at home?
The obvious answer is cost. For the price of some mastering software, you can create

your own production masters ready for duplication. The more important advantage to mastering at home is educational. At any level, it's advantageous to learn mastering terminology, techniques, and possibilities. After you've mastered a few of your own projects, you'll not only have a better idea of what the mastering process entails, you'll look at the entire recording process differently. You'll set levels, equalize, use effects, and probably arrange and orchestrate differently. You'll operate according to insider information; you'll see the final picture more easily, even from the first recording of the first note. After completing several projects from the recording of note one to the mastering of the last track, you'll find that your tapes need less and less mastering. They'll be closer to perfect than they ever would have been if you hadn't experienced the mastering process yourself.

What's the advantage to sending your work out be mastered by someone else?
Competitive edge! When you record music

that you feel strongly about and think is competitive, you owe it to the music to get a second opinion. Mastering engineers are the recordist's link to the real world. Once your project is complete and mixed, it's comforting to hire an engineer who has mastered successful albums that you think sound good. It gives your hard work a better chance to be held as worthy relative to its competitors. I've sat through several mastering sessions with a handful of the best mastering engineers in the business, and, even though I've learned a lot through the process, I still prefer to hire someone else to master.

If you want to pursue mastering as a passion or vocation, or if you just want to get good at it for your own use on your music, go for it. But how can you develop the skills needed to do a good job of mastering? Good mastering engineers have an excellent set of monitors that are efficient throughout the audible frequency range. They also have an accurate and stable monitoring environment. Their studios sound good and there isn't a lot of change in them throughout the months and years. Since this is the final stage before product production, be very fussy about the details. All components and cables should be the very best possible quality, and the wiring and implementation of all equipment should be meticulous and professionally done. Practice! Listen to everything you can get your hands on in the environment where you'll be mastering. Anything you master should sound great in comparison to your favorite albums. It doesn't have to sound the same, but it still should sound very good.

Acoustic Considerations

One of the essential factors in successful mastering is a finely tuned, finely designed listening environment. If your control room has inherent acoustical problems, everything you mix in it will have frequency problems. Acoustic problems are consistent, so they can usually be repaired during mastering. If your studio has a deficiency at 150Hz and 600Hz, you're probably putting too much or too little of these frequencies in every mix you complete. This typically makes the mixes sound bad in the car or in your friend's living room, for example. One of the primary values of a mastering engineer lies in his or her ability to compensate for bad mixing rooms.

No matter what gear you've amassed, if certain acoustic considerations haven't been addressed, you're going to have a rough time getting world-class sounds. When you make decisions about mastering—the final sonic molding of your valuable music—you must make those decisions based on an accurate listening environment.

Somehow, your studio must be broken up acoustically. At home, most of us operate in a bedroom-sized recording room that acts as a studio, control room, machine room, mastering suite, storage room, maintenance room, office, and possibly bedroom. The disadvantage of this setup is that you can't spread out into areas that are optimized for a specific purpose. The advantage is that you probably have a lot of stuff in your studio—stuff that absorbs, reflects, and diffuses sound waves.

Though you might have a lot of furniture and gear in your studio, additional help should be considered. Shaping the space around your recording equipment is clearly advantageous, especially in a room that is acoustically live. Live acoustics are good when they're been designed to enhance the acoustic properties of a voice or an instrument. When acoustics are randomly active, they are potentially destructive and must be controlled.

Physical structures within the acoustic space provide the best confusion of otherwise detrimental waves. Though soft surfaces dampen high frequencies, the low-mid and low frequencies (below about 300 Hz), which can be most damaging to sound, must be trapped, diffused or reflected in order to insure a smooth, even frequency response.

After hanging absorption panels on the studio walls and using tools like the Acoustic Sciences Tube Trap or baffles to confuse standing waves, the sounds you record are easier to mix and the mixes you construct possess sonic integrity. All of a sudden, your recordings sound more like the hits you hear on professional recordings. To overlook these considerations is to create a troublesome situation for your tracking, mixing, and mastering sessions. Address these issues so your music can have the best possible chance of impacting the listener with the power and emotion you know it deserves.

Monitoring

Speakers

Monitors are fundamental to the mastering process. If you plan to master your own music, select high-quality monitors that are accurate and consistent. Good, highly respected, self-powered near-field monitors are usually the best choice. Self-powered monitors are most consistent over several hours of use. Since the amplifiers and crossovers are at the speaker, they receive a line-level signal. Typically, the mixer's control room output plugs directly into each monitor. In this setup, the signal is then sent at line level to the crossover to be split into carefully selected frequency ranges. Once the signal is split, each frequency range is sent to its own amplifier—the amp sees the line-level signal and efficiently sends it to the speaker. Self-powered monitors contain amplifiers designed and adjusted to perform optimally with each component—and they sound good.

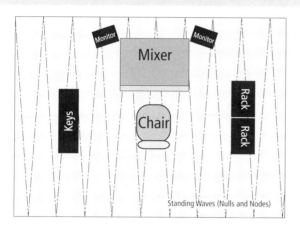

Standing Waves (Nulls and Nodes)

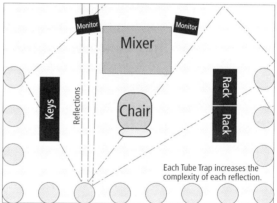

Each Tube Trap increases the complexity of each reflection.

The room on the bottom uses tall cylindrical tubes constructed for absorption and diffusion of sound waves to minimize standing waves in an otherwise bleak acoustical environment. Tools like these and others are available from Acoustic Sciences Corp., among others. There are many acoustical techniques that strive for a controlled balance of reflection, absorption, and diffusion.

Non-powered monitors receive an amplified signal at the speaker input. The problem with this setup is that it becomes less accurate over long periods of use. Since the crossovers are getting a powered signal, they heat up. Once they heat to a certain point, they react differently, changing the monitor's sound. Though there are some excellent non-powered monitors, self-powered monitors are conceptually superior, especially for home use. Building a traditional monitor system that's custom designed, utilizing non-powered monitors along with a line-level, external 3- or 4-way crossover, and outboard power amplifiers has great potential for accurate pristine sound. However, this approach is out of the price and expertise range of most home users.

Volume

If your control room is acoustically accurate, monitor at 85–90 dBSPL. This is the most accurate range for the human ear across the frequency spectrum. To verify this without getting into high-budget acoustical measurement gear, buy a simple and inexpensive handheld decibel meter. Most of these instruments offer A and C weighting along with slow (average) and fast (peak) attack times.

C-weighting is optimized for a full-bandwidth source at levels exceeding 85 dB. A-weighting filters out the high and low frequencies and is optimized for lower volumes. The A-weighted scale more closely reflects perceived volume, whereas the C-weighted scale measures amount of energy (amplitude), which doesn't equate to perceived volume at all volume levels and frequency content.

Monitor levels of 85–90 dBSPL become unacceptable when the acoustical space is poorly controlled. The less acoustic integrity a room has, the softer you should monitor. At lower volume levels room acoustics are less detrimental to the sound coming from the monitors. However, even when monitoring at low SPL, there remains value in

Curve of Equal Loudness (Fletcher-Munson Curve)

The graph below charts equal loudness (in Phons) across the audible frequency spectrum. The column of numbers in the middle of the graph represent perceived loudness as surveyed by two scientists (Fletcher and Munson) at Bell Labs in the 1930s. Notice that only between 700 Hz and about 1.5 kHz does loudness equate to dBSPL. This graph indicates that loudness (Phons) equates most closely with amplitude (dBSPL) across the audible band between 85 and 90 dB, the recommended monitor level for critical listening. We also see that more low- and high-frequency amplitude is required at low levels (below 80 Phons) to perceive equal loudness. In addition, it is indicated that the human ear is most sensitive at all loudness levels in the vocal intelligibility range, between about 1 kHz and 4 kHz.

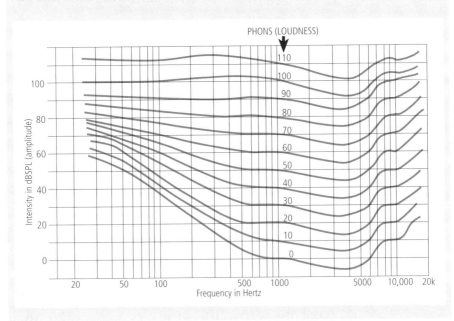

checking your music at a louder level just to make sure there isn't a glaring flaw, especially in the lowest and highest frequencies.

Digital versus Analog

Should You Use a Digital or Analog Source for Mastering?
Unless you're producing vinyl records, at some point the final product to be submitted for replication will end up in a digital format. That doesn't necessarily mean the entire source chain must be digital. Analog is still a preferred audio format because of its silky-smooth warmth, and many producers print their final mixes to $\frac{1}{2}$" analog tape. When I mix I print all audio simultaneously to multiple digital formats and to $\frac{1}{2}$" analog tape running at 30 ips. In mastering, I listen to each format to evaluate the emotional impact of each. A large majority of the time, the analog mixes just sound better.

Solid-state Clipping versus Tube Distortion

Waveform A represents Waveforms B and C before they were electronically distorted.

Solid-state distortion (Waveform B) has a harsh and irritating sound. Signals that surpass maximum electronic amplitude limits are simply cut off (clipped).

Tube distortion reacts in a more gently attenuated, rounded off fashion (Waveform B). The waveforms aren't clipped. They're acted on more like an extreme limiting effect. Even though the waveform is still distorted, the resulting sound is warmer, smoother and less irritating than solid-state distortion.

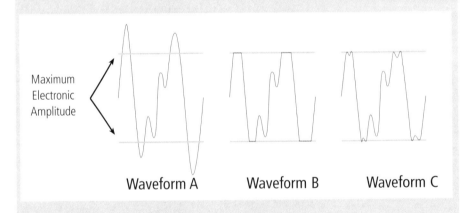

Maximum Electronic Amplitude

Waveform A   Waveform B   Waveform C

The sonic qualities of the analog format transfer well to the final digital master. The sound of the tubes and tape is much smoother and warmer than the sound of the solid-state and digital circuitry, especially when they reach the point of saturation.

It is the engineer's responsibility to know the sonic character of each tool available. If you know the personality of the tools at hand, you'll be better equipped to achieve the best results possible. Your choices will be informed, educated, and respected.

Mastering to Error Correcting Recorders

True random-access media, like hard disks, optical cartridges, WORM drives, etc., provide better and more accurate data transfer than sequential digital media, like DAT recorders. DAT recorders use an error correction scheme to fix occasional chunks of bad data. These corrections represent deviations from the actual data and, through multiple generations, accumulate in a destructive way. Though each correction might not be audible, it is inaccurate. It could manifest as a problem somewhere in the chain from your original master to the final product, especially if error correction is involved at several stages throughout production.

These errors explain the generation loss phenomenon of DAT recorders. In the early days of DAT, we were told that the digital copies were so exact they could be called clones. But error correction does not create exact clones! Listen to Audio Example 1; it demonstrates multiple-generation DAT copies of a digital master. Listen to the sonic character of the music as the generations increase. Listen for definition changes, image shifts, EQ discrepancies, and general changes in impact.

Errors

It's not practical to expect error-free digital recordings. There's always a chance of imperfections in the media or momentary noise interference with the flow of data. An environment with an ideal signal-to-noise ratio doesn't eliminate the chance of errors. Although it might minimize errors, it offers no guarantee that they won't happen. Error correction schemes offer a way to overcome error problems, often in a way that restores the data to its original form. However, certain repairs are merely approximations of the original data. These schemes explain the change in audio quality associated with multiple digital copies, especially in the sequential digital recording mediums like DAT.

In the digital domain, two types of data errors occur frequently: bit errors and burst errors. Occasional noise impulses cause bit inaccuracies. These bit errors are more or less audible, depending on where the error occurs within the word. Errors in the least significant bit (LSB) will probably be masked, especially in louder passages. On the other hand, errors in the most significant bit (MSB) can cause a loud and irritating transient click or pop.

Tape dropouts or other media imperfections, like scratches on a disk, can cause errors in digital data flow called burst errors. Burst errors, like bit errors, are potentially devastating to conversion of data to audio, especially considering that they represent larger areas of data confusion.

Data Protection

Given that errors are certain to occur, a system called interleaving is commonly used to minimize the risk of losing large amounts of data. Interleaving data is similar in concept to diversifying investments.

If you spread your money between several investments, there's little chance you'll lose it all. Similarly, interleaving spreads the digital word out over a noncontiguous section of storage media. That way, if a bit or burst error corrupts data, it probably won't corrupt an entire word or group of words. The damage will only affect part of the word, and the likelihood is great that correction schemes will sufficiently repair any losses.

Interleaving happens at both ends of the digital recording process. From A/D, converter data is interleaved as it stores on the media. Just before the data is returned to an analog form, the interleaved data is reconstructed to its original form. This clever scheme provides a system that is completely faithful to the original data, while spreading the risk of damaged or lost data.

Other correction schemes such as parity, redundancy, concealment,

Interleaving

The interleaving scheme inputs the samples into a grid in numerical order. Once in the grid, they're then sent out in a way that redistributes the sample order. Whereas the samples enter the grid in rows, they exit the grid in columns. Since sequentially consecutive samples are physically separated during storage, any disk related errors probably won't catastrophically damage audio quality. It is, however, imperative that the samples are put back into their correct order before playback.

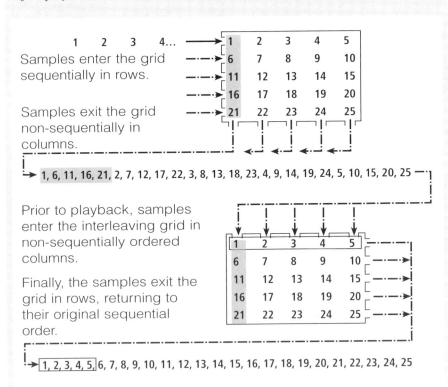

Samples enter the grid sequentially in rows.

Samples exit the grid non-sequentially in columns.

1, 6, 11, 16, 21, 2, 7, 12, 17, 22, 3, 8, 13, 18, 23, 4, 9, 14, 19, 24, 5, 10, 15, 20, 25

Prior to playback, samples enter the interleaving grid in non-sequentially ordered columns.

Finally, the samples exit the grid in rows, returning to their original sequential order.

1, 2, 3, 4, 5, 6, 7, 8, 9, 10, 11, 12, 13, 14, 15, 16, 17, 18, 19, 20, 21, 22, 23, 24, 25

interpolation and muting, along with interleaving, act to help insure the most accurate data storage and recovery process for the selected media.

Digital Modeling

Antares has developed several innovative products. Their microphone modeling systems lets the user dial up the vintage microphone of their choice. Simply plug any mic into the input, tell the processor what type of mic you've plugged in, and select the mic sound you'd like to hear from the device output. Microphones are popular tools, but they're very expensive— especially the classic vintage models. With a microphone modeler, more recordists have access to the warmth, beauty, and smoothness provided by the most sought-after microphones.

In addition, Antares and other manufacturers are continually coming up with digital models of vintage classic tube gear, new high-tech equipment and even the sound of analog tape. For those who have functioned throughout the development of the digital era there is a certain irony to spending hundreds of dollars on a plug-in to recreate the sounds of the mid-1900s.

Cabling Considerations

Some Cable Theory
An in-depth study of cable theory involves a lot of math, quantification of minuscule timing inconsistencies, and a pretty good grasp of quantum theory. However, basic understanding of a few concepts provides the foundation for good choices in cabling.

A cable recognizes a signal as voltage (electrical current). Small voltages travel down interconnecting cables (line level, instrument, data) and relatively large voltages (currents) travel down speaker cables. A magnetic field is created in and around a conductor as it passes electrical current. Any materials that optimize the accuracy of this conductance help the accuracy of the transfer process. Any design that takes into consideration the full-bandwidth of audio signal relative to frequency, time, and content, becomes complex—more complex than simply connecting a copper wire between the output and input.

Once a few manufacturers addressed the effect of cable on sound, it became apparent to those who truly cared about the quality of their audio work that cable design makes a difference. Most inexpensive cables consist of a conductor that's made of copper strands and a braided shield to help diffuse interference. Not much consideration is given to bandwidth relative to frequency-specific capacitance and potential frequency-specific delay considerations.

Two main considerations must be addressed in cable design: balance of amplitude across the full audio bandwidth and the time delays as different frequencies transmit throughout the cable length.

- *Balance of Amplitude*
  Monster Cable addresses this with their amplitude-balanced multiple gauge conductors. Because there are different depths of penetration into the conductor material by various frequency ranges, certain conductor sizes more accurately transmit specific frequencies. Therefore, it's implied that optimal conductance is accomplished by conductors that match the bandwidth penetration depth. With the frequency range divided among multiple types and sizes of wire, each frequency is carried in an optimized way.

- *Timing Considerations*
  High frequencies travel at a higher rate than low frequencies throughout the length of a conductor (wire). Low frequencies can't be sped up, but high frequencies can be slowed down by

winding the high-frequency conductors to create inductance at those frequencies. When the windings cause the correct inductance at the specified frequency bands, all frequencies arrive at their destination in accurate and precise timing and phase relation. This corrected phase relationship restores the soundstage dimensionality, imaging, and depth. When the frequencies arrive out-of-phase, they exhibit time-domain distortions of phase coherence and transient clarity.

All the major cable manufacturers vary slightly in their opinion as to how best to handle audio transmission through a cable. However, there is agreement that cabling is a major consideration. As end users, it's our responsibility to listen to what they to say. It's our job to listen to the difference cable makes and determine the most appropriate cabling choices for our own situation. Not everyone can afford to outfit their entire system with the most

expensive cable on the market—I realize
that some have trouble justifying even one
expensive cable. But the more serious
your intent in regard to excellent audio,
the more you should consider upgrading.
Upgrade the cabling in your main monitoring and mixing areas. Procuring a
couple of very high-quality cables to connect your mixer to your powered monitors
is an excellent place to start. If you use a
power amplifier, get the best cables you
can afford from your mixer to the power
amp and from the power amp to the
speakers. It'll make a difference in what
you hear, and therefore on all your EQ,
panning, effects, and levels.

Do Cables Really Sound Different?
The difference between the sound of a
poorly designed and a brilliantly designed
cable is extreme in most cases. If a narrow
bandwidth signal comprised of mid frequencies and few transients is compared
on two vastly different cables, the audible
differences might be minimal. However,

when full-bandwidth audio, rich in transient content, dimensionality, and depth, is compared between a marginal and an excellent cable, there will typically be a dramatic and noticeable difference in sound quality.

Listen for yourself. Most pro audio dealers are happy to show off their higher-priced product. When comparing equipment, its usually best to use high-quality audio that receives industry praise for its excellence. After all, that's the standard you are trying to meet or beat.

Young recordists are usually happy to get a system connected any way it'll work. To dwell on whether or not the cable is making any difference somehow falls near the bottom of the list of priorities. However, once the rest of the details fall into place and there's a little space for further optimizing, cable comparison might come to mind. In the meantime, we wonder why we can't quite get the acoustic guitar to sound full with smooth transients. We wonder why our mixes sound a little thick when we play them back on a better system, and we wonder why our vocal sound never seems as clear as our favorite recordings. We save a few dollars on cable while we make sure our mixer and effects are the newest and coolest on the block.

In reality, we'd be better off to build a system out of fewer components connected together with excellent cable. There are several very good cable manufacturers. Check with your local dealer to find out who's making great cable. It's not cheap, but it affects everything you do: how you mix, how you track, which effects you choose, and how you apply equalization— to mention a few. If the cables that connect your mixer to your powered monitors are marginal in quality, you'll base every decision concerning the sound of your music on a false premise.

Listen to Audio Example 2. The acoustic guitar is first miked and recorded through some common quality cable. Then it's recorded through a microphone with some very high quality Monster Cable. Notice the difference in transient sounds, depth, and transparency.

Audio Example 2
Mic on Acoustic Guitar Using Common Mic Cable then Monster Studio Pro 1000 Cable

Audio Example 3 demonstrates the difference in vocal sound using marginal mic cable first, then a high-quality mic cable from Monster Cable. Notice the difference in transient sounds, depth, and transparency.

Audio Example 3
Vocal Using Common Mic Cable then Monster Studio Pro 1000 Cable

The previous examples demonstrate the difference cable choice makes on individual instrument tracks. These differences are magnified in the mastering process when the entire mix is conducted from the source to the final replication master. In mastering, wherever signal passes through cable, get the best possible cable for the job.

Digital Interconnect Cables
Digital Interconnect cables also have an effect on the sound quality of digital masters and clones. Listen to Audio Examples 4 through 8. In each example a different cable and format configuration is demonstrated.

Listen specifically to all frequency ranges as well as transients. Also, consider the "feel" of the recording. Often, the factor that makes one setup sound better than another is difficult to explain, but it's easy to feel. The following examples use exactly the same program material as well as the identical transfer process to the included CD.

The differences you hear on your setup depend greatly on the quality and accuracy of your monitoring system as well as your insight and perception. Once you understand and experience subtle sonic differences you'll realize the powerful impact they hold for your musical expression. Constantly compare and analyze the details of your music. It will result in much more competitive quality. You'll realize more satisfaction and you'll probably get more work.

Audio Example 4
AES/EBU to DAT Using Common Cable then SP1000 AES Silver Digital Monster Cable

Audio Example 5
S/PDIF to DAT Using Common RCA Cables then M1000 D Silver Digital Monster Cable

Audio Example 6

Analog Out to DAT Using Common XLR
Cables then Prolink Studio Pro 1000 XLR
Monster Cables

Audio Example 7

ADAT Light Pipe into Digital Performer Using
Common Optical Cable, Bounced to Disk

Audio Example 8

ADAT Light Pipe into Digital Performer Using
Monster Cable's Interlink Digital Light Speed
100 Optical Cable, Bounced to Disk

If you can't hear much difference on some of these comparisons, try listening on different systems. Try auditioning several different monitors, power amps, or mixers with your own system. Keep in mind that there is a substantial cost difference between cables. It's entirely possible to spend more on the cable connecting two devices than you spend on either device, or maybe both devices.

With a budget in mind, choose to connect your basic ingredients with the best
cable possible.

Waveform Differences Between Cable

*In both of these sets of waves, the top wave was captured digitally through S/PDIF
using M1000 D Silver Monster Cable and the bottom wave was captured using a
common RCA cable. In case there's a doubt about whether the cable really matters
in an audio environment, these comparisons speak very graphically that they do.
If the transfers were identical in data, they'd look identical.*

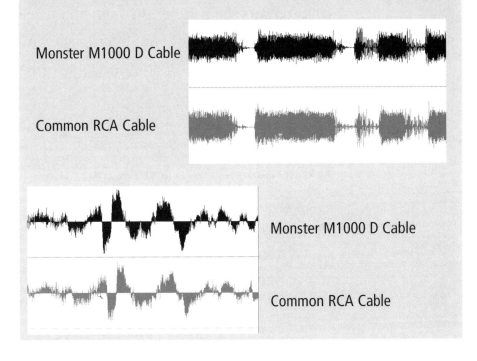

Monster M1000 D Cable

Common RCA Cable

Monster M1000 D Cable

Common RCA Cable

Cable differences are often so extreme that they can be seen in the onscreen waveforms. The illustration above shows two identical waveforms: one recorded through a common RCA cable into a digital S/PDIF input, while the other utilized an M1000 D Silver Monster Cable.

Assembling the Album

There is an art to assembling an album so that it draws the listener through all the songs. When all songs have been placed in an artful order:

- The album is easy to listen to as a complete work.
- Each song leads gracefully into the next.
- Contrasts in texture, tempo, and lyrical content hold the listener's interest.
- All material plays to the same audience, so your intended audience can relate to everything on the album—there

aren't a couple tunes that seem out of place.

A good mastering engineer thinks of the flow of an album. Spacing between songs might be adjusted to hold interest or contrast textures. Throughout the course of an album, the level of the songs might increase to help hold attention, or the limiting might increase to make the songs seem progressively louder. In this way, the momentum of the songs seems to increase slightly, although the level of each song is still optimized. As the mastering engineer you must listen for perceived volume; don't merely look at signal levels. At the identical amplitude, a simple production consisting of minimal or no instrumentation and one voice sounds much louder than a full production. The mastering engineer must compensate for these variations in musical density.

Spacing is easily adjusted during mastering, but it's often best to listen to the entire album several times to determine if the spacing flows well with a natural momentum. Therefore, spacing between songs is often best determined prior to the actual mastering session.

Equalizing

Equalization is an important part of the mastering process. Each song must sound compatible with the progression of the album. If one or two songs are deficient in low frequencies, or if a song or two lacks high end, they'll stand out over the course of album play. Each song has to sound like it belongs in the kettle with the rest of them.

Variations in EQ are common from song to song, especially when a project is completed of the course of several months. Equipment changes, tastes change, and skill levels change throughout the progression of any album. Try to mix all songs on the same monitors and in the same studio; it'll make life easier during mastering. Once a studio owner changed the weighting of the woofers without telling me, just before I mixed the final song of an album. When the low-frequency response changes dramatically, the resulting effect on the mix is very graphic. Once you get into the mastering studio, it's obvious that something went suddenly astray. The song I mixed on the woofer-altered speakers sounded like it had been mixed on a different planet compared to the other ten songs on the album. Fortunately, since the deficiency was global, the mastering engineer was able to pump a substantial amount of low-end into the song. In the final product, it flows very nicely with the other songs. You'd never know there was any problem with the mix.

Find a specific recording that you think sounds great. A group held in high esteem by the recording industry provides a strong example to compare your mixes to in each session. If you reference each mix to the same recording, you'll have a good chance of creating mixes that flow well together. When referencing mixes to confirm your mix integrity, listen to the low frequencies and very high frequencies especially. Listen to how transparent the mix sounds in the midrange.

Air

Most of my favorite albums have an excellent and controlled high-frequency content. The frequencies around 18–20 kHz are subtle, yet they add greatly to the feel of a mix. Inclusion of this frequency range often referred to as "air" gives a mix an open feeling—a perception that the sound isn't closed in.

Highs

All frequencies are important when mastering, but without solid, controlled high frequencies any song can sound dull and lifeless. Too many highs create a brittle and harsh sound.

Mids

We often concentrate so much on high and low frequencies that we forget the importance of mid frequencies. A mix with controlled and balanced mids is typically very warm, smooth and easy to listen to. This is also the frequency range that's capable of placing a sonic cloud over any mix when in improper balance.

De-essing

Often, in the tracking and mixing process, extreme compression techniques overexaggerate vocal sibilance. When this happens, a de-esser is necessary to bring the sibilant sound back under control. A de-esser is simply a very fast, frequency-specific compressor that can sweep the high-frequency range to locate problem sibilant sources. The de-esser must be set carefully to only bring under control the exact frequencies causing the problem or it will rob life from the music.

Lows

Low frequencies often provide the greatest challenge. They contain the most energy of any frequencies and, when too powerful, can produce an artificially hot mix level, which results in a quiet-sounding track. A good mastering engineer crafts and molds the low frequencies to create a master that is powerful yet controlled for optimum impact.

Audio Example 9
Reference Mix (No EQ)

Audio Example 10
Air Increased then Decreased at 18 kHz

Audio Example 11
Highs Increased then Decreased at 5 kHz

Audio Example 12
Mids Increased then Decreased at 400 Hz

Software versus Hardware Equalizers

Many engineers are very attuned to their analog equipment and only prefer to use their hardware. This is an excellent approach when every part of the signal path is meticulously designed and crafted. Keep in mind that the quality of your audio is dependent on the integrity of the least common denominator. With that in mind, home users are often destined to find the best software and work digitally within their computer.

Many excellent software packages are available for both the Mac and PC platforms, like T-racks, Spark and many others.

Real-time Analyzer (RTA)

Some engineers like to mix while referencing a real-time analyzer (RTA). This tool displays the level of specific frequencies across the audible spectrum. I've seen engineers that couldn't use the restroom without consulting their three-dimensional RTA. To top it off, their mixes didn't always sound that good. If you use a tool like the real-time analyzer, consider that it is just a simple tool designed to help. The true test is in the listening. A song can look mighty fine on the analyzer yet sound like garbage, or it might look bad on the analyzer and sound great. There's always the possibility it'll look good and sound good. I love it when that happens!

The RTA divides the audible frequency spectrum into regions—typically 31 regions, correlating with the 31 bands on a ⅓-octave graphic equalizer. Each region is represented by a series of LEDs, which indicate the region's energy level in the same manner as the audio level meter on your mixer or recorder. A good mix is typically flat across the spectrum, with a little roll-off at the very top and bottom of the frequency spectrum.

The RTA receives its signal in one of two ways:

- Through a calibrated microphone
- Through a direct line input

Acoustical RTA Measurements

Use the microphone when checking the frequency integrity of your monitoring environment. If you set the microphone at the same position where you monitor the mix, then play pink noise through the system (all frequencies at an equal level) you should see each band on the RTA at the same level. If you see an abundance or a lack of certain frequency bands, you have a couple of options:

- Make changes in the mixing environment, which will affect the acoustic character. Physical construction isn't always the easiest route to go, but, in the end, it's often the best solution. If you tune your studio so it's accurate, you'll be able to trust that your work will transfer favorably to the rest of the world.
- Hire an acoustics consultant. It could be the best money you spend on your studio.

If your acoustical problems are insurmountable, try inserting a 31-band graphic equalizer between the output of your mixer or computer and in inputs of your monitor system. A $\frac{1}{3}$-octave graphic EQ (31-band) correlates directly with the bands on a real-time analyzer. If you have a predominance of energy at 500Hz, simply turn that frequency range down on the RTA until it registers flat when the calibrated microphone hears pink noise through your monitors at the mastering engineer's position. In this way, it's possible to get a room to register properly on the RTA, but it's not always preferable. Simple equalization is accomplished through filters and phase-altering circuitry. These circuits have the potential of causing more problems in your listening environment than they're fixing. The importance of this connection dictates the use of very solid and sonically transparent EQ. In other words, it's not cheap.

Electronic Evaluation of Frequency Content
A real-time analyzer also receives a line-level input. Many mix and mastering engineers prefer to connect a send of the source to an RTA to evaluate frequency content across the audible spectrum. This tool helps quantify what you hear. Most commercial mixes contain a fairly even balance of frequencies throughout the duration of the song with a slight roll-off around 20 kHz and about 60 Hz. With the advent of higher quality consumer audio equipment the highest and lowest

frequency have become more and more practical to include in a mix. As a mastering engineer, it can be comforting to actually see that the frequency content of the final master is consistent across the spectrum and that there are no obviously glaring peaks or dips in the curve. However, some of the very best mastering engineers never use an RTA; they rely on their ears.

Levels

During the mastering process, mix levels are a primary concern. Optimizing levels is important during the mixdown process, but mastering is the place where the final adjustments are made in regard to the level, flow, and momentum of the entire album.

It's technically gratifying when each song on an album reaches maximum level at least once. However, some songs just sound louder when there are set to maximum levels than others. The ideal in the mastering process is to keep the levels maximized while at the same time creating a complete work that sounds great throughout its entirety.

Normalize

Normalizing is the easy way to move all the levels up to the point where the peak(s) hit maximum level. In concept, this helps insure that song levels are as hot as they possibly can be and that the full word is being used (the maximum number of bits). However, it should not be an automatic move to normalize every song on an album.

Young recordists, often without thinking, normalize each song. I don't see that happen when I sit with some of the best mastering engineers in the business. What I do see is careful evaluation of the song, the sound, the style, the content, the character, and so on. Careful consideration must be given to the intent of the artist and to the music's audience. A plan should be developed for the impact of the album as a whole.

Normalizing isn't necessarily a bad thing to do, but it shouldn't be automatic. There are often other means that create the proper levels in a more pristine and musically desirable way.

Real vs. Apparent Levels

A song's level seems obvious, right? Either it's maximized or it's not. In reality, it's not that simple. Frequency content, instrumentation, and orchestration all play a part in how loud a song sounds. If your album contains a wide range of instrumentation, from full band with strings and horns to voice and guitar or even just voice, you'll need to evaluate the volume of each song in relation to the others. You won't be able to count on normalizing every track, that's for sure.

The fewer instruments involved in the mix, the louder it'll seem at maximum levels. Have you ever noticed how full and punchy basic tracks sound before all the synth and filler parts have been added? It seems that the song sounds softer and softer as you put more and more into it.

Tasteful limiting and compression can help even out the levels, but simply using your ears to find the levels that flow best from song to song is also a good plan. If you have level questions throughout the album, be sure to listen to the entire album on several different systems. What might seem like the perfect relationship between tracks in your studio might seem distracting and inconsistent in your car. It pays to check the level relationship in as many separate environments as is possible. One value of an experienced mastering engineer is the accuracy with which these adjustments are made.

Limiting: How to Sound Loud

The peak limiter can be your friend or your enemy. Most mastering engineers use some degree of peak limiting to help control sporadic peaks and to help keep the overall level of the album as high as possible within the constraints of taste and style. Keep in mind that, if your peak limiter registers 6dB of limiting some time during the mix, you can boost the level of the entire mix by 6dB to reattain maximum levels. Therefore, your song will sound 6dB louder. That's an amazing difference in volume.

Typically, the best mastering results are accomplished using a multiband limiter. Dividing the frequency range into two or three separate ranges, which are limited separately, produces the most punchy and consistent sound. However, as the individual bands limit, they change in their relative levels to each other. When highs, mids, and lows are limited separately, there is potential for adverse impact on the sound you toiled over. It's a good idea to use limiting in moderation. The best plan is to mix with mastering in mind. If you create your mix so it maintains constant levels, and if you're very deliberate and precise in the development of your sound, there'll be less need for limiting. The mastering process might include slight peak limiting, which is used primarily to keep a lid on the level to insure against levels above digital maximum. This way, more integrity and control lie in your hands from the onset of the project through its completion and duplication.

Overuse of limiting creates a sound that is thin and lacking in life. When the entire mix stays at maximum level throughout the song, there's no release. Transparency, contrast, and depth are lost. Even the best multiband limiters lose punch when they're pushed too hard.

How Hot Is Hot Enough?

Throughout the course of each album, levels should reach the maximum several times. Some recordists like to leave a decibel or two of headroom in order to avoid overdriving the electronics of older CD players. That's not what I see happening in the real world. I see levels being pushed to the max, and then I see some peak limiting. Then I see levels pushed to the max again. It seems like everyone is trying to get the hottest mix on the planet. I've heard mastering engineers recommend pushing the digital levels over maximum.

This aggressive approach isn't appropriate to all styles, though. It's inappropriate for most jazz, classical, bluegrass, gospel, and country western albums. Your understanding of the style you're working with should guide your decisions in mastering.

Listen to Audio Examples 14 through 17. The same mix is played with three different limiting levels. The first is normal, as mixed. The second demonstrates 3dB of limiting, and the third and fourth demonstrates 6 and 9dB of gain reduction. Remember that once the gain is reduced on the limited portions, the levels are brought back to optimum, where the strongest section peaks at zero on the digital meter.

Audio Example 14

Normal Mix

Audio Example 15

3dB louder WAVES L2 Ultramaximizer

Audio Example 16

6dB louder WAVES L2 Ultramaximizer

Audio Example 17

9dB louder WAVES L2 Ultramaximizer

Software versus Hardware Limiting

I use an excellent hardware multiband limiter patched between the digital mixer output and my CD recorder input. I use this primarily for printing reference mixes for the artist and myself to evaluate outside the studio. I like its sound but I've never used it to create the final master for replication. Software, designed for mastering application, is very trustworthy and more quantifiable than many hardware limiters for home use. Again, there are excellent renditions of both hardware and software mastering tools, but most of what creates great masters is the subjective musical decisions made by the engineer.

The CD Mastering Environment

There's more to preparing a CD master than simply digitally recording and spacing ten or so songs in the correct order. The format must be correct for the application. Codes need to be correct, verified, and confirmed. Protocol must be followed to insure proper duplication and replication.

In order to effectively operate in a CD mastering environment, make yourself familiar with its language. Absorb the specialized terminology that pertains to mastering alone. Be sure you know what the replication facility expects to insure the best possible outcome for your music.

Write Modes

There are two basic modes used to write an audio CD:

- *Track-at-Once Mode*
  This mode writes a track at a time. The laser is turned off and put to rest after each track, after the lead-in, and before the lead out. This system lets the user record song after song in different sessions and at different times. The material doesn't need to be recorded all at once in track-at-once mode. When the laser is turned off, small areas are left

unrecorded on the CD media. These unrecorded sectors, called runout sectors, are perceived as corrupted by the player. While many CD players are able to skip over the corrupted areas, CD readers at the duplication facility are likely to view them as errors. Track-at-once offers the advantage of letting the user write more audio data to the CD in separate sessions until the CD is full. This mode is best left for less-critical projects like quick references, compilations, or archiving mixes. Track-at-once CDs do not meet Red Book standard.

- *Disc-at-Once Mode*
  This mode writes the entire disc, including the table of contents, lead-in, audio data, and lead-out, in one continuous pass. The laser is never turned off and there are no unwritten, or runout, sectors. This mode is the professional standard for the creation of a CD master. Disc-at-once mode conforms to Red Book standard.

Red Book

Sony and Philips defined the Red Book standard (in the form of an actual red book) for playback of digital audio CDs (CD-DA). They also defined various formats for audio, video, image, and data storage. Each standard was released in a colored binder, hence the terms Red Book, Orange Book, and so on.

The Red Book standard defines the proper format for an audio CD to play back on a CD player, and it defines the format for a CD player to play back a CD. Any Red Book–compatible CD can play back on a commercial audio CD player.

The Red Book standard defines the number of digital audio tracks on the CD as well as the type of error correction used to guard against minor data loss. The standard calls for up to 74 minutes of digital audio, transferable at the rate of 150KB per second.

Red Book standard requires certain specifications be met:

- Each track must be at least four seconds in length.
- All track numbers and index times must be unique and in ascending order.
- There must be a minimum Index 0 gap length of four seconds.
- The maximum number of tracks is 99.
- Index 0 must always be at zero seconds.
- Index 0 of the first track must be between two and three seconds in length. In other words, Index 1 must start between two and three seconds after Index 0.
- The disc must be finished. In Disc-at-once mode, the data is written from beginning to end without stopping; the laser isn't turned off during the write process. The table of contents, lead-in, audio data, and lead-out are written continuously and in order. This process conforms to Red Book standard.

Each CD track typically contains one song. Tracks are divided into 2,352 byte sectors that are $\frac{1}{75}$th of a second long.

If a disc is scratched or dirty, Red Book standard specifies an error detection code and an error correction code (EDC and ECC), so the player can recreate the music according to code.

Most commercially produced CDs conform completely with the Red Book standard, which is also called the Compact Disc Digital Audio Standard. A disc conforming to the Red Book standard usually says "Audio CD" under the Disc logo.

Scarlet Book

The Scarlet Book contains the standard for Super Audio CD (DSD) format. Scarlet Book specifications include the option for three different disk formats: single-layer DSD, dual-layer DSD, and a dual-layer hybrid which also contains A standard Red Book CD layer that is functional on a standard CD player.

Yellow Book

The Yellow Book contains the standard for CD-ROM. When a disc conforms to Yellow Book standards, it typically says "Data Storage" under the Disc logo.

The Yellow Book standard emphasizes accuracy for data storage. Whereas an audio CD operates peacefully within an error correction scheme, errors in data storage easily render a file or application useless. Error–free schemes are essential for storage of computer data.

The Yellow Book augments Red Book protocol by adding two different types of tracks: CD-ROM mode 1, for computer data and CD-ROM mode 2, for compressed audio and video data.

Green Book

The Green Book is the standard format for CD-I (CD-Interactive). This standard was designed for multimedia applications that play in real-time, combining sound, images, animation, and video. The CD-I format and the playback unit associated with it were designed to use an inexpensive computer and audio disc player along with an ordinary NTSC television as a monitor.

Orange Book, Part I and II

The Orange Book standard defines the format for write-once CDs (CD-WO) of both audio and CD-ROM data. The Orange Book specifications are designed so that a Red Book compatible CD can be created on a write-once disc.

Part One of the Orange Book specifies the standards for magneto-optical systems that use rewritable media (CD-MO).

Part Two of the Orange Book standard defines the CD-Write-Once specification (CD-WO). The standard divides the disc into discrete areas, each for a specific function. The Program Calibration area is used for a test run to calibrate the recording laser. The Program Memory area is used to record track numbers along with their stopping and starting points. The Lead-in area is left free to write the disc's table of contents after all data is completely recorded. The Program area is where the actual data is written, and the lead-out area is placed at the end of the disc to let the player know when to stop reading.

White Book

The White Book standard represents the fourth major extension of the Red Book standard. It is a medium-specific standard allowing for 74 minutes of video and audio on a compact disc in MPEG format. The Sony/Philips Video-CD (VCD) is White Book compliant.

Blue Book/CD-Extra

The Blue Book/CD-Extra standard stores Red Book audio in the first portion of the disc and Yellow Book data in the second, completely separate section. Since an audio CD player is a single session machine, it only recognizes the audio session, since it is first on the disc. CD-ROM drives are typically multisession devices, so they see both the audio and data sessions.

CD-Extra, originally known as CD-Plus, solves many of the problems originally encountered with enhanced CDs.

PQ Subcodes

All audio CDs have 8 channels of subcode information interleaved with the audio data. These subcodes serve various functions, depending on the actual digital information being stored. Some codes apply specifically to audio, some to video and graphics, and others to MIDI data. The subcode channels are identified with the letters P, Q, R, S, T, U, V, and W.

Channels R–W are used to store video information on CD+G discs, or MIDI information in CD+MIDI discs.

Audio CDs use only the P and Q subcodes. The information on the P channel tells the CD player when the tracks are playing and when they aren't. The Q channel contains much more information, including copy protection and emphasis information, track and disc running times, disc catalog code, and track ISRC codes.

IRSC Code

The International Standard Recording Code (ISRC) uniquely defines each specific track on the CD with information about the song's author, the country of origin, and the year of production. The ISRC can be written directly into the CD's Q subcode channel. Each track on the CD can have its own unique ISRC information.

Emphasis

The emphasis flag in the Q subcode alerts the CD player to activate the de-emphasis circuitry in its analog output. Early CD players had poor quality digital-to-analog converters, so CDs were recorded with a pre-emphasis, high-frequency boost. Emphasized CDs must be played back through an analog de-emphasis circuit to insure accurate EQ.

Converters have improved dramatically over the years, and emphasis is no longer necessary; it's rarely, if ever, used. However, when source material is utilized that was originally emphasized, it must be de-emphasized in playback.

SCMS

The Serial Copy Management System (SCMS) resides in the Q subcode. It allows the audio to be digitally recorded once but prevents second-generation digital copies. When the SCMS flag is present, it is en-coded in the data stream when a digital copy is made. If the SCMS or Copy Prohibit codes are inactive, unlimited copies can be made from the source. Whenever distributing your material on CD for review, select SCMS or Copy Prohibit to help insure against piracy. However, these schemes don't offer much protection, since it's child's play for an adept tech-head to break the copy protection scheme.

Track Number

Each song or contiguous audio segment on a CD is called a track. There can be up to 99 tracks on each CD, numbered from 1 to 99, always in consecutive, sequential order. A CD can start with any track number from 1 to 99, allowing for continuous numbering of tracks in multiple CD sets.

Indexes

Each track on a CD can contain up to 100 marked locations, called indexes, within each track. The indexes, numbered from 0 to 99, are always in consecutive, sequential order. All tracks contain at least one index. Index 1 defines the start of the track. If there is a gap of silence after the previous audio ends and before the actual audio data begins, it's labeled as index number 0. All other index points are optional and user-definable.

There are two types of indexes: absolute and relative. Absolute indexes calculate and display all times relative to the beginning of the CD. Relative indexes calculate and display all times relative to the beginning of the individual track that they're indexing.

Noise Shaping

Noise shaping is an option that is sometimes present in the dithering process. Noise shaping utilizes digital filters to remove noise that falls in the middle of the audible spectrum, typically around 4kHz—the human ear's most sensitive range. Since noise is actually important in the control of quantization error, it isn't completely removed through noise shaping but is, instead, shifted to a range which is harder to hear. Noise shaping lessens our perception of the noise essential to the dithering process.

Image Files

When it's time to create your CD master, it's usually preferable to create an image file from which the actual CD master will be made. Any good CD mastering software provides a means of creating an image file. When an image file is created, all the songs and segments are copied to a contiguous section of one of your drives. When you create a CD from files that are scattered all over your drives, there's opportunity for inaccuracies and errors to creep into the data flow. However, an image file is an accurate and continuous copy of all data. When the CD master is created from an image file, the data flows smoothly and freely onto the disc. The transfer can take place with

Sound Advice on Mastering

greater accuracy and at faster speeds. When printing from an image file, it's better to print the master at faster speeds because the data will be backed up and bogged down at slower speeds.

The image file was originally used to facilitate the use of slower CD burners, but it offers a way to make smooth and accurate data transfers and provides a means for trustworthy archives of all audio data in a project.

Summary

Mastering is a key part of the recording process. It is an art which requires a lot of decision making and it's always best if those decisions are made according to some serious experience and an accurate listening environment. Take the information and suggestions contained in this book and practice mastering. Master a song and then listen to it everywhere you can. Make notes on anything you hear that could make the song sound better. Then go back and remaster to see if you can beat your first try. If you have some friends who would enjoy helping with the process, test your mastering out on them. Either master their music or have them critically evaluate yours.

This is an art that greatly benefits from a sonically accurate room and from meticulous electronic installation of very good gear. Wire matters. Power matters. Experience matters. Musical taste matters. The longer you master music, the more you have to offer in the process.

Learn to be a musical chameleon. Don't hang on one style. Learn what they all sound like. It just isn't right to master everyone using the same amounts of limiting, equalization, etc. Jazz is obviously different from rap, like western is different from metal. The more musically informed you become, the better job you'll do on a wider range of projects.